MISS DESERT INN

poems by

Ron Salisbury

Winner of the 2015 Main Street Rag Poetry Book Award

MAIN STREET RAG PUBLISHING COMPANY
CHARLOTTE, NORTH CAROLINA

Library of Congress Control Number: 2015948621

ISBN: 978-1-59948-535-5

Produced in the United States of America

Main Street Rag
PO Box 690100
Charlotte, NC 28227
www.MainStreetRag.com

Acknowledgments:

My thanks to the editors of the journals in which the following
poems first appeared:

> *Acorn Review*: "1943"
> *A Year in Ink*: "Three Stitches"
> *California Quarterly*: "Angel"
> *Eclipse*: "Dog Waltz"
> *Hiram Poetry Review*: "Miss Desert Inn"
> *San Diego Poetry Annual*: "Ginger"(now "Elegy"), "Vacation,"
> "The Black Psalm"
> *Serving House Journal*: "Not the First," "Hearing Aids,"
> "Entre Chien et Loup," "Severance Pay," "Gloria"
> *Soundings East*: "The Chiaroscuro of Divorce"
> *Spitball*: "The National League Playoffs Are a Form
> of Self Pity"
> *The Briar Cliff Review*: "One Last Try for Perch"
> *The Cape Rock*: "Memorial"

My thanks to Steve Kowit and Sydney Brown; the Pier Writers
at the Lazy Hummingbird: Lloyd, Charlie, Imant, Maggie and
America; the Not Dead Yet poet's workshop at Writers Ink. For
their diligent attention to early and final drafts of this book: Allen
Clark, Anna DiMartino and Jackleen Holton-Hookway. And
extraordinary thanks to the Heart's Desire Poetry Gang, Christina,
Dorianne, Kim and Laurie, where it all started.

for Steve Kowit

Contents

THERE'S SNOW IN HEAVEN

JOSEPH AND THE MIRACLES

THE SHORT LIVES OF MEN

LINWOOD SALISBURY

Gloria

Ron Best loaned me his girlfriend
for the Junior prom. She graduated
two years before from another school,
had a job and great tight sweaters.
She held her Lucky Strike like a pencil,
blew smoke out her nose, didn't drink beer
but carried bourbon in her purse. I would
have been in love if it hadn't been for Ron.
On the slow dances, she'd snuggle in my neck,
her hands on my butt. "Are they all watching?"
she'd ask.

It had been a bad year. Dumped by two girls,
each one, I knew, was the one. Stretched
out ahead would have been the house
squared with the lawn, white stake fence,
steady job, two weeks off in the summer.

I didn't know it then, but I was on the edge
of Brewer, Maine. The last dive off the cliff
to New York City, then the swim through the surf
toward the rest of my life.

Ron's girl pushed her Marilyn brassiere
against my sport coat lapels, her face
in my neck. Later, as I delivered her
to Ron's waiting car, she whispered,
"If he ever dumps me, you're next."

And I've been looking over my shoulder
ever since, after every divorce.
Would the cigarettes have got her,
the bourbon? Or, would we be
in some town an hour from the opera,
her teaching English, still tight under
the sweater, and me trimming the hedge,
the grass a perfect green dream,
our afternoon tea in its cozy, steaming.

Jazz In Low Rooms

Paul Bowden, hunched on the manure
spreader's high seat, worked the family
field in the droll sunset, clods
and funk twirling up behind him
in the peach and ochre striped horizon.
Maine farms grew rock and pumpkins,
blackflies, gnats in spring, the best jobs
at the pulp mill, hardware store
if you were really lucky. You married
Sally Ann Condon and that was settled.
Drank a little more each year, a little more
after each kid, there was no saving
in Maine, just endurance. Hope
was what you used to get through.
No escape, ever. Every lost job
was just the Penobscot mud
sucking you down. Each divorce
was Sally Ann squinting over a sink
of dishes, the diaper pail. Hope
made a sound like a rubber boot
pulled out of the stanchion muck.

Paul grew up with the Berlin
from the National Geographic,
at the end of an air tunnel, planes
back and forth with food, coal, underwear,
brioche. The Berlin in news reels,
in black and white noir films with hopeless
lovers in sooty doorways, the wall
at the end of the street, fedoras,
long fawn skirts and seamed hose,
bright red lipstick on unfiltered cigarettes,

whispering *Paulie* in his ear, the jazz
in low rooms, the soul's Armagnac.

The bus left Bangor because it had to,
and Paul, twelve rows back, window seat,
also. The bus left Bangor because it had to,
relieved him of the last act, the going,
he only had to get on; New York City,
Baltimore, the Far Coast. No more
farm, but the jobs felt the same,
a Sally Ann on every bar stool, you just
dragged your life to a new place,
same manure.

After November, 1989, unification,
the news at six showing them dancing
on the wall, the Brandenburg Gate,
a peach and ocher glow in the late Sunday
afternoon. Paul, hunched on a stool
in a Van Nuys bar, swore he'd live in Berlin
someday. Probably lucky he didn't because Berlin
was very different from his Berlin
where the grocer, (do they call them that?)
helped him with the words for morning bread,
sweet and yellow, and later, evening bread,
seedy and braided, where to find
the coffee roaster, how to say "lamb chops."
His house is shaded by large deciduous trees,
chestnut or locust, (do they grow there?)
the bay window opens on the sides
and you can hear the children coming
and going to school, (what is the word

for school—schulen? schulisch?) jabbering
with pinched juvenile larynxes, giddy
with guttural words, waving to him
as he writes at the table knowing that later,
the third wife will return from the embassy
in time to watch the last bits of sun
drip through the green chestnut filigree,
polish the blood wine in the thin
tall glasses they hold up to the light
that dapples the sidewalk outside,
that doesn't exist.

1943

At the Eastern Star Fall Formal
some jerk kicked my mother's chair.
A heap of yellow crinolines, legs out
and everyone rushing to help.
Nine hours later I was born, yelling,
pissing, and nothing much has changed
for me since. In January, before
that October, it's always cold in Maine,
in their little two story, World War II
raging outside. Father's a traveling salesman,
bad back, bad kidneys and mother's raising
my sister, the meager meal always hot at six.
Was there much hope in Orrington, Maine?
In the world that night? Would there ever
be enough meat and sugar again?
I like to think it was hope, not dread
or the cold that pulled them together
after doing the dishes, dialing off the radio.
It would help to know I came from hope
that night, not dread.

Driver's Education

In 1953
my father taught me to drive
in the hundred acre hayfield
beside our farm
a decades old Ford
choke and spark
on the steering column
silver starter button
on the floor
mechanical brakes
which were like no brakes
to a boy of ten
who had trouble reaching the pedals
you pushed the floor shift
into neutral
middle of the "H"
grabbed the bottom of the steering wheel
stood with both feet
on the brake pedal
which didn't stop the Ford
in time twice
straight through mother's
sweet pea trellis
front wheels in the tomatoes
two weekends rebuilding
replanting promising
Oscar saying Edith
leave the boy alone
he's got to learn somehow

Linwood Salisbury

was struck by lightning twice, only one was fatal. Standing in the
open doors of the barn, the summer squall crawling across the two
hundred acre hay field, the downpour slowly sweeping toward him,
a crease across the plump grass, now past the crab apple tree in the
middle, thrashing leaves and limb ends around and Linwood didn't
notice his toes were on the iron pipe halfway sunk in the ground that
served as the guide for the two big rolling doors. First his hair floated
out as though under water, then he noticed the metal buttons on the
bib straps of his overalls glowing. "Very peaceful," he told us later;
the glowing, the hair. Then out of the corner of his eye, a whitening
beginning to the right of the open door that grew and washed over
him like a soft, big hand. He woke up in the dark twenty feet outside
on his back. "Damn near drowned," he said. "All that rain in my open
mouth. And me out for God knows how long." Although barely forty,
his brown hair turned dandelion weed white, haloed his head just like
one, wouldn't stay down. His hazel eyes grew milky blue. "Not much
else changed," he said. Except we all noticed how much quieter he
was, took a long time answering. "Well, sumptin like this happens,
makes ya kinda think." Stopped reading the Bible at night and started
listening to the Red Sox on the scratchy local radio station, the only
baseball you could hear in Otis, Maine. Quit eating meat, except for
white perch. And bourbon tasted good now. Tore out his cornfield
and put in raspberry canes, pumpkins between the rows. He lined
a hundred carved and candle-lit along his gravel driveway the last
two weeks of October. No kids ever came to his home to trick or
treat, that long scary walk by those pumpkins and Linwood with a
bowl of jujubes, his dandelion hair backlit in the doorway. Two years
later, after milking his six Guernseys at four, sitting on the empty hay
rick seat just inside the open barn doors, watching a summer squall
inching across his field, he thought this was like stories he heard
about World War II, soldiers jumping into new bomb craters because
they knew another one wouldn't fall in the same spot.

Bikini

A chain link fence between
his back yard and Ada Moran's
kept her dogs from crapping on
the snow in winter that after melt,
appeared like foul pimples on the lawn
in spring. It also discouraged Ada
and her casserole experiments
from appearing at his back door
every week or so; Ada had designs
and Elwin wasn't in the market.
Why not a six foot solid redwood,
thought Elwin, why'd I let
that Sears salesman talk me down
to chain link as Ada moved her chaise
to the fence edge and stripped
down to a little black thing
no seventy-five year old woman
from Maine should wear.

East Orrington Congregationalist Church

Wilbur Cotton went to church each Sunday
to rinse out Saturday night. Three Feathers
Whiskey still puddling his brain, not too sure
what he'd done this time but knew, for sure
it wasn't good. At least he woke up looking
out his dormer window not the jail cell door.
Blessings, Wilbur thought, blessings for another
week. Safe in his favorite pew he knew
the preacher preached to him, ignoring
all the others, raining down invectives,
threats and promises about his soul.
Most men are lost, Wilbur felt, lost
and floundering on Saturday's shoals.
I've got lots of company, thought Wilbur,
and none of it is good.

T. R. Savage and Co.

My father was a grocer,
not the run-a-store kind
but sell-the-goods-to-the-store
kind. Really, a traveling salesman,
worked for Boutelle Savage
for thirty-five years until
Boutelle sold out
to the Hanaford Brothers,
shave-tail upstarts that fired
all the old guys, like my father,
pruned the client list, dumped
all the small family stores
in the north east section
of Maine.

Every Monday, father,
in his trim double breasted, stiff
starched white shirt, Bay Rum,
Lucky Strike in the corner
of his mouth, leather satchel
filled with flyers for deals,
order forms, new leads,
would pull out early
in his Sunday washed Buick
to start his route. Sometimes
gone a few days, especially
if he had to go to Machais
or Calais, right near
the New Brunswick border.
Lunch at the same places
where the other briefcase guys

would meet; Kendall Oil,
Mossy Meats, John Deere
equipment, a livestock vet,
joking with the waitress,
telling road stories and lies,
coffee and cigarettes.

After I was born,
he wrote my mother letters
from the road, how he couldn't wait
to get home to the both of us.
When I was ten, sometimes
he'd pull me out of school
and we'd head north, Machais,
Calais, two days on the road;
two guys. In those lunch-time
diners, the waitresses always
poured his coffee first, sometimes
ran their hands along my cheek,
"He's a fine one, Oscar," they'd say.
"One fine boy." I'd wait in the car
while he paid the tab, leaning across
the counter, close to her ear, her
hand smoothing his lapel.

It was like the night coming early
in winter and he still had chores
to do when they let him go. No more
work in Machais, no diners. No
waitresses. No suits. The weeks
closed in like channel grips. Trade in

the Buick, a pickup for spot work,
the first heart attack, the second.
Dusk at first, then night. Mother
at the hospital leaning over
to smooth his pajama collar.

Bucksport

I thumbed   a ride home   from New York City   but only got
to outside Lewiston   in the rain   the cold drenching down
the phone booth   I was hunched in   the occasional Bangor Aroostook
line of boxcars   dieseling north   maybe   I should have tried
to jump one   but I didn't know how   the hours   limping through
the night   like the eighteen wheelers   lurching   onto the on-ramp
that wouldn't stop for this guy   racing out   to thumb them down
in the rain   Bucksport   that wood spool factory   pulp wood mill town
on the Penobscot they cleaned up   stopped   dumping acid and sulfur
when they "blew the cook"   and the salmon   came back
big runs each spring   sushi bars   wine bars   money   from Boston
Victorians into B and B's   locals moving to Dexter   because local rents
went through the roof   lived here all our lives   and can't afford
a craft beer   now   can't find a cowboy bar   anymore
with a drunk drummer   Dick Cotter on vocal   and a consumptive
lead guitar player   named Larry Glish.

Royce Bowden

Hard at work he was, grease
and barked knuckles, maybe blood
and viscera, feathers, gristle, a tight

bandage on one finger,
Royce Bowden fought through
his sophomore year then gave up,

married Edith who dropped out
the year before, who was already
pregnant anyways, and stared down

a narrow road, nothing possible
beyond the gullies at the edge.
They started first upstairs

at the uncle's house, Edith
with all the laundry, meals, the place
was never this clean and Edith

was not that good. When Royce
got the extra shifts at the slaughterhouse,
bought the old truck with the plow

from his cousin and contracted
with the town for clearing the roads
in winter west of Brewer Lake, all

the way to Kings Mountain, they moved
to the apartment above Moran's
general store. Then back to the uncle's

when the truck gave out, the baby
just a few months old, the uncle grinning,
"It'll cost ya this time." Better food,

more cleaning, iron his overalls and he got
to watch Edith nursing the baby. And this
was the best part of that narrow road,

gullies filled with raging water. Two more
babies, Royce found whiskey to his liking,
the slaughterhouse shutting down every now

and then when the business sagged, the uncle,
in his chair across the small sitting room
from Edith and the newest kid, her blouse

pulled aside. This is where we leave Royce
and Edith. This is where I leave Snows Corner
Road, Orrington, Maine, Kings Mountain, Brewer

Lake, South Brewer, Bucksport, the uncle,
the slaughter house. This is where I catch
the bus west to New York City and start

down my own narrow road with its ditches.
Time makes a sound like racing water in culverts
beside the roads, Even 13th and Avenue B

is a narrow road, Pyzynski's Luncheonette,
pierogis, kielbasa and breakfast deals
line the gullies. Even the west coast,

Sunshine Launderette, Fu's Market, Hoosie's
vanilla egg-creams all line the gullies
you can't step over. Berkeley funnels

its run-off into the San Francisco Bay.
The ocher and peach light drains down
the felt hills and oak crotches

to the road edges in Sonoma county.
No one is exempt from history.
Likely Royce is dead or close to, maybe

Edith too. God help the children. Dying
takes a lot of attention. Even this, we all
just wanted a life, even reduced to this.

Oscar

She told me her name was Etro
and she had loved my father,

the grocery salesman with two
kids, a plump wife and assorted dogs.

Somehow she ended up in a diner
in Machias, Maine; a waitress,

who hemmed her skirts short,
eye shadow, got her perfume by mail.

Trapped far from the sunny piazzas
where you wear your best red

lipstick and flirt with the boys
in the sticky summer nights.

Father was the closest
thing to romance in Machias,

twice a week on his route for years,
Winston in the corner of his mouth,

big lapels of his 50's gray double
breasted, Bay Rum, starched collars.

A swagger, a line polished by years
of imagining someone like Etro.

"You have a brother, you know,
his name is Carlo, tall, like he was."

Hidden Poems

When I knew Aunt Ida,
her tall back was stiff.
Bunned gray hair pulled tight.
Her settee and chairs
covered in plastic, the piano
not played anymore.

Her roommate for decades,
Miss Fahey was small
and thin as a winter sparrow,
the soft to Aunt Ida's oak soul.

From these fifty years
in the future, I look back
kindly now; I think of sorrow,
stuck in Bangor, Maine,
behind the doors of that
second story apartment
over the green grocer,
reciting poems to each other
by Edna St. Vincent Milay.

Severance Pay

Francis Abbott lost three on the right hand,
not the thumb or pointer finger. Lucky, because
you got to keep your job if you still had two.
They paid extra to work on the chipper, more than
you could make anywhere else with a high school diploma
in South Brewer, Maine, in the 1950s. The Eastern Paper Mill
had the best jobs in the area, but the cost was high.

Uncle Ed knew the foreman and two weeks after graduation,
I was on the line, pulp hook in one hand, feeding four-foot chunks
in the hopper, cotton balls in my ears. I helped pull Francis
out of the blades.

At Benny's Bar across the street, after the 4 PM shift change,
you'd find the chippers lifting a cold Narragansett with only
two fingers, teasing a peanut out of a bag with the thumb.
If you were crazy enough to work the line, you were old enough
to sneak into Benny's for a beer, no one questioned
the underage kid with a scraggly moustache.

The afternoon I caught the Greyhound bus to New York City,
I stopped in to say goodbye to the guys. They all understood
when someone wanted to leave while still whole. The lot of them,
on their stools saluting me as I left, one, two fingers
to their foreheads.

One Last Try for Perch

The lake is a broad rock in the cloudless night
that curls from tamarack on one shore to red
yellow maples on the other. The fall bites
and bruises through my thin frock coat.
I am seventeen with tomorrow stuck
in my throat. My father, hunched over

his rod in the boat, wants to surprise me
by saying something important, a last tough
bit of belief that would make me want to hug
the rural life he finds sharp and constant.
But I am bound for the blue dog of ruin
in New York City and he knows it.

Tomorrow I catch the bus west to rub
the tough leather of risk and he will watch
the cool blue wavering exhaust and clutch
his chest over his heart, wondering if he should
have tried a hug or kiss instead of fish,
instead of the mud of New England reserve.

After the Last Long Dance

Over the Ford's hood, the fresh daylight
reaches into the lake like two fingers
touching a top button in the last smoke
from the summer moon being winched
down behind hills across Brewer Lake
where Rachael Jack stretched across
the front seat, her sweater open
clear down to possibility, the lowing light
a moan on his hand wrapped around
her thigh below the plaid green skirt
plowed high like last winter's snow curled
in the ditch by Royce Bowden's plow
at 5 am, Royce squinting into the white bugs
of snow pelting the plow's windshield white
as Rachael's navel in the wrung out morning,
the radio's gold dial playing Donovan
to the tilted belly button aching
for a tongue to sample last night's dab
of Avon lotion promising to make her his
or him hers, if not forever at least until
the green field of skirt is jimmied up
like a stuck window into each others' future,
one night way beyond tonight, maybe
one of them in Maine still, the other
an ocean west or further before each
crawls alone beneath a single plaid
duvet, hair now snowy
splashed into the long past night's lake.

Macys, Herald Square, New York City

Lithuania, the radio commentator says,
could be at risk. He goes on to explain
the Russians but I went back to
the first time I heard the word.
Lithuania, she lisped, because English
felt like a strange peach in her mouth,
she said. Lithuania, I grew up
in Lithuania. Everyone was drinking
too much, talking too loud, music,
a siren on Avenue B, cabs hissing
by on the wet pavement three floors
below, hard to hear, and I just wanted
to hear her say anything, read
the label on the bottle, dictionary,
say my name. God, just say my name.
Once again for coffee, the last time
when I brought her a lupine
where she worked selling women's gloves.
The worlds then were not just language
but spun around different suns. I was
just out of the Maine countryside,
she seemed to have floated down
from some lofty plain. In the fifty years
between Lithuanias, how would it be
now. Would the spheres spin closer
now, run our fingers down the lines
in each other's face, laugh at what
happens after selling gloves. Or,
would there be anything left at all,
because Lithuania, the announcer says,
is at risk.

THE ANGEL OF LAS VEGAS

Out Of Egypt

Two snails trailed the exact slime outline of Egypt on the patio in Las Vegas, late at night, the sprinklers swish, swishing on the lawn, the yellow overhead bug light lemoning the concrete slab, the moon a balloon over the nearby vacant desert lot and Jim Kosicheck and I, stoned, very stoned, ready to fall down in God's awe—what else could explain Egypt, until Rene, Jim's wife, leads us inside and shush, shushes us because the kids are asleep, God knows what we two would have done, although, if I'm truthful, this was not all that strange during my eleven years in Las Vegas, the sun hot as a pizza oven, before dope was a social problem and we all practiced being cool with martinis and looked for something, maybe God, in everything—why Egypt if this is not the Bible talking, it could have been the outline of Nebraska, Ethiopia, but Egypt, for God's sake, the blood of the lamb on every door, snail slime on every patio, what is happening in all the other apartments with no snail slime in this complex, the youngest being taken by that wrathful God and I won't go home tonight, I'm safe sleeping on the couch and Rene makes Jim and me coffee in the morning, fixes the kids breakfast, loads them in the station wagon for school, then grocery shopping, the cleaners and Jim and I discuss the possible mayhem, the loss in each apartment in this complex, then light up a big one and consider the marvelous ways of God or someone or at least Ron Branvick who sold us this dope then decide to call Brent Price and describe the snail trails, ask what he thinks and he hangs up—what the fuck—two beers later Brent is at the door seemingly concerned about our spiritual life until he samples the Branvick dope and soon we three orient ourselves at three points on the patio, flat on our bellies, trying to find the trail of Egypt, the sun, now almost a hundred and one, sweat in our eyes and Rene, patient Rene, home from delivering kids, groceries, finds us awash in the glow of God, or maybe on the hearth of Shadrach, Meshach and Abednego's furnace, trying to find Egypt on the patio to save us all.

Tropicana Hotel

They used to say statuesque
before the silicone days,
when only the few got to Las Vegas,
feathers and a G-string,
a few brief years for God's
fabulous freaks that the guy
with a garage door business
in Minneapolis carried home
in his mind for those winter nights,
the little wife, or not so little
wife, whipping up mac
and ground beef, the two kids
hating each other over homework
at the kitchen table. And the guy,
pushed back in his recliner,
hockey on the tube with that showgirl,
all feathers and little else
beside him saying, "What'll it be,
big boy?"

Now, anyone can be statuesque
including the barkeep slinging ice
in a shaker in front of me, the slice-
necked black tee shirt with *Beer Flirt*
on the back, the statuesque part
will still be there when she's forty.
And that guy in Minnesota,
whose business can buy the science
but not the feathers,
and something's just not right.
In January, pushed back in his recliner,
beef sizzling in the kitchen, little wife

lurching back to avoid the fat drops
down the front of her bulging T-shirt,
the Red Wing's center slap-shots
the winning goal and it just feels so flat.

Needles

Tony Albenese wouldn't wear platform shoes when platform shoes were in, "Tried 'em once," he said. "Made me look like a short Sicilian standing on turtles." Tony, who conned me out of fifteen hundred for a deal he had, but I'm ok with that because we'd hang out in casinos and he'd tell me stories, two twenty dollar Keno tickets in his hand that paid off now and then. How he invented the electronic poker slot machine, but he wasn't connected enough to keep it; the big boys took it away, Frank at the Tropicana who ran the town, Bilbray, the Clark County assessor, Frank's mule. "I got ideas nobody's thought of, Ronnie boy. Nobody." Tony, who'd call his wife on the bar phone. Ask her. Not tell her. Ask her to come over for a drink because he knew he was into me for fifteen and his wife always wore something very low-cut and liked me. Would always give a real tight hug. Tony, who got his start in LA with topless bars when topless bars were something new. Had no money, he'd tell me, stiff the contractor until he was ready to sue then pay him off with cash from the till, let a girl sit on him in a booth on the dark side of the bar. Pay the liquor guy after two trips, who was his own crook anyways, with cash borrowed from the girls, promised them ghost raises, the late shifts when the drunks paid off, asked how their kids were doing in school. Marked the bottles so the bartenders would know how to short pour, taught the girls to watch the door man for the OK, no cops in the house and the booths on the right side were the darkest. "Every one," Tony said, "looks great in mesh stockings and weird lights. Don't ever come in during the day." Tony, who set up the slot joint at Sahara and The Strip with someone else's cash, a big crazy neon sign on the roof but talked too much when they took it away, Frank and his mule, Bilbray. Tony, whose head, after I moved to California, only his head, was found in Needles, California, six months later.

Gravel

She walked across
the parking lot
to her four by four,
a country gait,
foot in each furrow,
long dancer legs,
slightly spavined
from pliés, ginger
pony tail,
a metronome
above the body's pistons.
I know love
when I see it.

How I Got My First Earring

Showgirls in Las Vegas are not allowed
extra pounds or tan lines which makes
summer pool parties with no clothes
and white wine spritzers.

On one of those summer days that feels
like a forge, twenty people around the pool
in the fenced back yard being beaten
into a stew by the sun, some of us dumb

from too many spritzers, the teenage boy
next door mowing and mowing and mowing
the same patch of grass by the slatted fence,
and Danny Dowd, a boy dancer, walks by

wearing only one earring. Jan rolls over,
her breast between my arm and chest
and whispers, "I'd really like to see you
with an ear ring." And thirty minutes later

some lady in a department store jewelry section
is holding a gun to my left ear. At the time
it seemed a good idea and later when Jan got home
from the last show at the casino, it was a great idea.

A Hymn to the Clavicle

Clavicle, she said and I said, clavichordium? She said, no,
clavicle, that little bony shelf my breasts hang from.
You know, she said, the Minoan women of Knossos painted
theirs bright red, like eyebrows above their bare breast
eyes, so they could see exactly what they wanted. Right here,
she said, the collar bone, what Billy Betts broke
when we convinced him to jump off the rabbit hutch.
He'd like to touch mine if he were here, if he were lucky.
She unbuttoned the top three, pulled the shoulders down,
the Napa sun dripping down our sides, the sweet salty sweat
puddling, squeezed a lime wedge along that bony ridge,
handed me a shot of Patron, tilted her head back,
the black floppy hat an umbrella above a drink, her big dark
glasses reflecting my approaching tongue. Right here, she said.

Miss Desert Inn

I wouldn't buy a new car,
kept the old one because
after the movies, last show,
the Las Vegas summer night
still eighty-seven degrees,
she liked to ride twenty minutes
up the sloped east valley side
until the lights on the Strip
twinkled like a miniature
Christmas village,
then pull off on a dirt schist
path and fuck on the car hood,
our flimsy summer clothes
hung over the rolled down window,
banging the Chevy hood flat
in just the one month of August.
Then everyday driving to work,
the market, that scrunched hood
or the memory of that hood,
has stretched out for forty years
before me, pulling toward
some disappointing treacherous
duplication ever since.

Napa

Not breakfast
often an afterthought
or dinner
too important
but lunch
under the full potential
of the hot noon day
air heavy
the ficus trunks wound
around
leaves simmering
in the slight breeze
the vines drip
with promise
a glass of Chablis
three thin slices
of chicken
two of avocado
capers
Muscat reduction
later
soon
the loosened belt
the slip of nylon
down the thigh
the sun on the vines
the sun
Mozart softly
the heart the heart
with no promise
adagio adagio
the afternoon oiling

into ocher light
wonder
consequence
one strawberry held
up for her to bite.

Three Times

My father, who wasn't a fisherman,
tried to teach me to fish for white perch
in Beech Hill Pond where we had
a cabin he built on weekends so we
could fish. One big shed roof rectangle,
three bedrooms, a long room overlooking
the cove, knotty cedar paneling
he stripped and trimmed from small logs
in his workshop, water from the lake
hand-pumped into the kitchen zinc sink,
an out house sixty feet in the woods.
When I turned fifteen and discovered
Rachael Jack, he sold the place
rather than argue about weekends.
He taught me as much about Rachael Jack
as he did about perch. In Maine, in the fifties,
the Korean War raging a universe away,
he did his best which wasn't that good
after all.

Mt. Charleston is an hour outside Las Vegas
where I married Jan who put herself
through college working
as a Folies Bergere showgirl, two shows
a night, dark on Mondays. Mt. Charleston,
cool above the brazier of the summer
valley floor, ten feet of snow in winter
where we bought a teeny cabin—showgirls
and stage-hands on summer Mondays painting
the walls, shingling, figuring the plumbing,
catching the high mountain sun on the outside
balcony, no tan lines these showgirls, glint

of telescopes and binoculars from across the canyon,
the girls hanging over the railing, waving—
that we sold to pay for her grad school
in San Diego where she left me, where I tried
my best, but, it wasn't that good
after all.

And Cobb Mountain above Clearlake, one hour
from home in Northern California, dirt road,
Ponderosas sissing the top branch wind.

A salt box, two stories, deck and tub out back,
two acres of forest floor. Three Christmases
where I taught Liz's three kids how to lay a fire,
get the wood stove to draw with a twist of newspaper
in the flue. Where the weekends away from work
could have been as far as Korea or Las Vegas
but not far enough from the end which took
the business, salt box, family, and me.

In the time left, there are only so many cards
in the deck and I've been dealt my share,
doubled down and split my tens when I shouldn't.
Three of a kind is a good hand, a lucky one.
You don't often get it when the pot is fat.

Oahu, 1973

Somewhere in a shoe box,
there is a photo of two six foot
Las Vegas showgirls on Oahu,
arms around a wrinkled Japanese
fisherman on the North Shore,
his surf rod gripped tight, barely
five foot, grin splitting his sun-brown
face: my wife, the one on the left.

Some snafu in scheduling
and the Folies Bergere
had to shut down for a month.
The casino sent everyone to Hawaii
to keep the show intact including
husbands, boyfriends
slathered in sun block,
wielding cameras, coupons
for luaus, free drinks at tiki bars.
No tops, just G-strings
for the girls, tan lines stood out
like raccoon eyes in klieg lights.

The entrance to the assisted living
has a planter pot on either side
of the front door, a poor example
of a Greek amphora, crudely crafted,
not like those pulled from the Aegean.
Each pot has a fake concrete cord
down the middle, pulling the amphora
into two long halves, a peach, I think,
or Jan when she bent over
to pick up a shell on Oahu's North shore,
the fisherman transfixed with his rod
held overhead as the fish swam away.

The Angel of Las Vegas

This was the age of encounter groups. 1972, when we all tried to find ourselves, our true inner beings. I was from Maine. I didn't know there was anyone else inside me. But my new wife was a psychology student and she had me try on every psychosis she read about, go to weekly sessions with the therapist Bernie who wheezed and sneezed through the whole hour and I never knew if it was the true me or the inner me he was allergic to. I went with her to every experimental workshop, Neuro Linguistic Programming, Reichian, Rolfing. I had my aura read, my irises analyzed for good health, and then this crazy workshop with two guys who could look at you and determine that your deep neuroses were blocking the energy flow in your body and rather than talking about the issue, they physically attacked the blockage which led to the guy with the beard, two hundred fifty pounds, bouncing on my legs, me on my back, legs up, feet pressed against his chest, him yelling "Push. Push. Break through. Free yourself." And pop! I could literally hear a pop. I limped out early and spent the rest of the afternoon in a nearby bar.

I think hernia procedures have become more refined since 1972. These were the times when you stayed in the hospital for three days rather than getting it done while you have the oil changed in your van. The Winter Olympics in Japan were on TV and the guy in the bed beside me had pain pills he'd share as long as my wife and her friends kept sneaking in late at night, between shows, to visit; she and her friends being showgirls at the Tropicana Hotel, this being my Las Vegas days and this being the way my wife paid for college. And the pills kept coming as long as one of the girls would let slip the top of her long coat so the guy in next bed would get a peek at her tits. Jan and her three friends lounged on my bed, one lying beside me on the pillow, full stage make-up, flesh meshed legs, folding, unfolding those long legs, the long coats barely buttoned, the doctors coming in to see if I was alright, the interns, the male nurses, even the security guards: was I alright? did I need anything? The skiers in Japan floating off the end of the ski jump like storks, bobsledders, skating pairs in thin outfits leaping axels, the slippery pain-pill haze, two martinis in Dixie cups the girls snuck in. It's getting late, they all take turns kissing me good night and clatter down the hall in their stage heels. The doped-up guy in the next bed leans back on his pillow, sighs and waits for the Angel of Masturbation to visit in a couple of hours.

THERE'S SNOW IN HEAVEN

There's Snow in Heaven

Three days at the Now and Then Motel
waiting for her to get here,
no cell phones, snow up to your ass,
so cold snot spikes in your nose
on the walk to the liquor store.
Bad cable, just four snowy channels,
two of them hockey, I hate hockey.
And I don't care if she's fifteen years
younger, thinks I know what I'm doing,
when I get to the bottom of this bottle,
I'm outta here, back to Florida
and the damn ponies at Hialeah,
palmetto trees, suffering humidity,
the sweat a glorious puddle down your back.
What was I thinking? It was
just a bad spot of luck, a month
without a real winner, no exactas,
daily doubles, just a few lousy shows,
and she's standing by the window
in a patch of hot Florida sun
wearing only a toe ring and says,
"Honey, when the going gets tough,
there's always Duluth. You go first
and I'll catch up." What was I thinking?

Angel

I'm tired of angels who just hang around
watching our troubled world, only report
the failures. I'm tired of angels with ice
on their wings who have to spend hours
warming in the weak winter sun before
starting work. But some of them
have ignored the arrogance that comes
with omnipotence and grovel down here
in the muck. Take mine, for instance,
she's tattooed her wings on her shoulders
for ease and a Harley insignia on her thigh
for the hell of it. She has a job in the day
pumping gas and at night tells me about life,
if she's not too tired. We talk a lot about love
because it's what she can't do. "It breaks
all the rules," she says. "And I'm already
on probation." "But maybe I'm falling in love
with you," I tell her. "I can stop it,"
she says. Pauses. "But I won't." "Why?"
"Because," she answers. "Love is what happens
when you can't take it anymore. You're not
the most exciting assignment I've had,
but at least you don't knock me around."

The Black Psalm

Thirty-two miles to Fort Bragg curved between the oak-jammed gullies,
cow hills and valleys for more than an hour where Madame ChiChi waited
to finish the tattoo stripe on my leg that covered the scripted name
of my first wife.

At fifty, I didn't then and do not know now why tattoos are so important
except to separate fifty from being fifty and the wet look of promise
my youngish new wife gave me as I grimaced on the table, Madame ChiChi
bearing down with a six wide needle singing black ink to my thigh,
the wife twisting my right nipple to balance the exquisite pain of significance.

Oh, fisher of memory, burden of ink, what carries the psalm of a life into the surf
of years crowded with bodies if not a road whirled between cow hills, redwoods
and the pain of that younger wife now living in Seattle and I'm not, the ink
ribboning the thigh, forearm and back, Madame ChiChi smiling
into some other guy's soul, his wife wrenching the nipple of memory.

Dog Waltz

I'm not working now, or rather, no one
wants my labor and this gives me time
to notice things especially on the early
morning walks when I usually see the same
one or three others tethered as I,
to a dog of great privilege. One
is pulled by a brute of a beast, then
a guy with a limp, dark glasses and furry
rat-like dog, another is a slim redhead,
no ring, that seems approachable were
it not for our slightly incompatible hounds,
all of us doing the dog waltz at 6 AM.
Before the day delivers what materials
it wants me to use, I could be anyone,
anywhere I've dreamed before whatever
went missing went missing. I could tether
the mutt to a tree and walk across Genter
Street and tell that slim redhead that it's time
we introduced each other, that since she always
wears a baseball cap, I really want to know
what her shaded eyes tell us, tell her
she's in my poem, and, "How about
a cappuccino for starters." But there's nothing
like divorce to reveal the fragility of wonder and sex
and the absolute truth about opera and baseball,
who really likes each one. We circle
our neighborhood, stop for a bagel, the privileged
dog gets half, and continue our route, same bush,
flower, corner of the brick planter. He never tires
of the messages left by his cronies. Perhaps
it is the same message from last month
and he is just memorizing it, a poem by some
talented, forlorn whippet two blocks over,
rhapsodizing about the shortness of life.

The Chiaroscuro of Divorce

at the polished
conference table
she twirls
the cloisonné locket

one side, the cranes
of Edo
the other, night

everything listed
in two piles
the two attorneys smile
with compromise

the dark air
is outside
the bright glow

of reason is in here
shaded in their eyes
I am undone
there is nothing

in my pile
I could not
live without

push the stack
to her side
and walk outside
to the quick air

night
is just
the light gone

Three Stitches

Not the gruff voice
leaping out of a doorway
at 2 AM with a Buck knife,
not the sharp rim
on the bonnet underside
of an antique Jag,
not the spike
from the broken plate
when the second wife left,
no kick from a rooster,
slip of a pearl-handled
boning knife at Thanksgiving,
a straight razor, shaving before
the awards, or the thin edge
of her zipper, after.
But trimming the root end
of a celery stalk before lunch
for one, the lonely sun smudging
the table, oil for the salad,
arugula, pico de gallo, avocado,
tomato. Henry Purcell's
Dido and Aeneas filling the room
like a dirge and I'm thinking
of us in Venice or was it
the Pegasus Vineyard in Napa,
the knife slicing through memory
like a quick dog catching a scrap.
A reminder to pay strict attention
to what I have now and leave
the rest for a time free from self-pity
and away from sharp things.

A Glass of Wine

When the check arrived in the mail,
it was more than expected. A short
walk to the bank, then the liquor store.

My patio is dusty and big enough
for one chair, tiny table, dog asleep
at my feet, the traffic a wasp in my ear.
A thousand miles south of where
I would be if I could.

A sip of the Pinot Noir, not expensive;
a fruit pastiche, blackberries, cherries
on the nose. It takes me north
to one of those flat bottom valleys
like corduroy whaling, inland
from the ocean, Petaluma,
Sonoma, Napa, and the deck
is still warm from the gone hot light,
our clothes tacky against our backs,
the cool Pinot a bowl of rubies
in the glass, the woman hard and soft,
and your heart a puddle in your chest.

4 AM on the Day My Ex-Wife Gets Remarried

Not the lamplighters who call out the night's wellness,
    but the others at dawn, someone to snuff out the flames.
        Derby hats, scarves, a steady job with the other early risers

—gutter sweepers, rag men, green grocer and his nag—
    starting at one end of the long block and dousing the night
        one wick at a time. The Specter in his ratty overcoat

and fingerless gloves lurks in a door stoop at the end
    of the townhome crescent, counts each snuffed light
        coming toward him. Angels have bells, he has his man

with a snifter on a long rod. He hears crying, a gasp, renting,
    negotiating, prayers that bring a shine to his bent face.
        Pennies for eyes as though that was enough for the journey.

No. At least a half crown for the toll. These are what the Specter
    uses each night before his vigil for the tumbler of gin,
        meat pie and Virginia Common in the clay pipe. Keeps count

with string knots in his pocket. From the third story window
    of one of the many mealy little flats they carved these grand homes
        into, a guy in a plaid bathrobe with worn spots, sits
            watching, writing

it all down. He needs a shave. A dog dream-twitching at his feet.
    Three fingers of bourbon in a cut glass tumbler. He catches the eye
        of the lurker in the ratty overcoat, gives him the finger.

Entre Chien et Loup

time at dusk, when a wolf
can be mistaken for a dog

In the fall
night appears
when we're not ready,
still have the crayons
out on the porch,
tamping the potting soil
around the dwarf lemon
on the balcony.
Not ready
for the light,
another day
to cartwheel away,
not ready
for another year
to cartwheel away
until we've rolled around
in its leaves again,
made the bedsprings
under the camp bed sing
once more. Are we ever
ready for night; greed,
we say, that's us. Desire,
like a shag rug we remember
by the fire place. Want,
we negotiate,
not the night pushing in
with his scythe.

The Brahms

The sun rolls down the afternoon,
spits up magenta and cochineal
on the undersides of low
clouds off the coast. On my
small patio, the dog has his head
on His bare foot. God points
with His fork at the sunset,
"That was a good idea." He
watches me peel the avocado.
"You're getting old. Shouldn't
you slow down? You're trying
too hard." No, I say. No. Slice
the avocado into thin crescents.
"Did you like the Brahms last night?"
He asks. Just ok, I answer. The
tall young woman in front
looked like my last wife. I couldn't
concentrate, everything sounded
alone. Squeeze a lime wedge
over the slices, a few sprinkles
of cayenne. God spears
a crescent with His fork. "This
was another good idea."
"I gave you three wives, wasn't
that enough?" No, I say.
No.

Janus

January is a hateful month,
just when you're not looking
it happens again, the Wolf Month,
the coldest time, Plough Sunday,
Robbie Burns Day. The pruning month,
not the apples and the apricots
but the crone in three cloth coats,
kerchief knotted under her chin,
two bags from the market,
one loaded with cat food, who keels over
in the cross walk slush; the old duffers
in galoshes and plaid caps with ratty
ear flaps half way down the driveway
with the snow shovel, face down
in the drift, the upturned heels
of their boots like two black grave stones,
the snow shovel straight up, a flag
to alert the medicos where they are.
They couldn't get to Florida, bad planning
when they were young, skimpy Social Security.
In Minnesota and Maine, a boy and his dog
always try to slip-slide too far out
from the shore on the new ice
and January sucks them down through,
the slow current taking them away
from the hole, their eyes watching
the blowing snow above the smoky ice
until the eyes marble over.
January, that bannister of knives
we slide down toward another damn birthday
and one more malady we didn't imagine
would happen to us. The hangover month,
It's not the beginning but the beginning
of another end.

Elegy

Gold fish in the toilet, rats beneath the agapanthus,
raccoons and Rosie the chicken, the old dog that disappears
and nobody asks where. Children need this, it's training
for what's to come. Few really "go gently into the night".
It's usually smelly, lavender and urine, begging for deals,
terrifying for everyone and those left behind,
if they would admit it, are damn glad it's over. In 1923
a department store in Tokyo caught fire and dozens
of kimono shop girls died because they wouldn't jump.
Beneath the kimonos, tradition held, you wore nothing.
A city law passed soon after decreed that shop girls
wear panties. When father died, mother, Mother
who couldn't write a check or pick her dress for the day
without father, sold everything, put down his stupid poodle
and flew to Oaxaca, a spot her finger landed on.
It all became clear when the embassy called us to claim the body.
Fifteen years ago I tattooed my back with a line from an e.e.
cummings poem; "how do you like your blue-eyed boy, Mr. Death."
And each year I run faster, a glance over my shoulder,
the dark clouds growing, anvil shaped, tornados, typhoons.
I can shave every morning and not look at my face. Just
a peek so I don't nick the chin but not enough to see
my father's face looking back at me. Who is this guy?
Why are his lips so thin. And the spots on the cheeks,
the floppy ear lobes, weird sprouting hair; bags and sags.
Children need this. They really do. Whoever it is, sell
my stuff, go to Mexico, don't kill my dog.

In The Year of The Snake,

my seventh decade slithers
through the dead leaf duff
toward me, lifts its wedged head
and squints rheumy eyes to see
how far to the next warm rock.

Blood cold serpent, wishing for
one more decade's sun, coil yourself
around the tan thighs of memory,
squeeze out that last wet drop.

God

Eight old writers were arguing about God,
whether the poet meant God's work
in his poem and not just some guy
on a bridge in a storm.

Across the room a young woman packed
in soft gray tights and a tiny top worried
her long blond challah bread hair
with tapered fingers, waiting for her coffee.

Often it's hard to deny God's presence,
the infinite patterns of wonder and design,
the unapproachable agony of His presence.
And sometimes it is in a poem.

Not the First

The first kiss suffered from bad aim.
I'm not sure about the second,
but by the third, purpose and target
were clear. Rachael Jack,
who still hammers my dreams,
taught me possibility,
revealed how soft skin was,
the tip of someone else's tongue
and the mechanics of a bra strap.
Thirds are best, I think,
they're filled with experience
not the raw spring of first leaps.
The third marriage was best.
The third dog, with buckeye honey
eyes, knew when I needed a lick
on my hand. The third car,
an orange 69 Camaro, moon roof,
attracted, among others,
Miss Desert Inn in Las Vegas.
The third home
had an oak spiral staircase
the third wife would slowly step
down with handcuffs in her hand.
You take your firsts, filled
with the fumble of innocence
and I'll wait for the third
who has two tattoos, a flask
of Bulleit bourbon and cash
from the Harley she sold.

Vacation

I got as far as Stockton
before the van gave out

not a long way from San Diego
but far enough

to remind me
this is not Stockholm

or Melbourne
Bonn or Berlin

where I traveled
when I had money

quit carping she coughed
at least youre with me

and I aint been
to those places neither

Hearing Aids

My hearing is not what it should be,
I don't mean just old man hearing;
it's a bit gone, dim, damaged. When
I first worked, no government agency
gave a shit, no OSHA, no worker's comp.
Just do the job, pay the rent, die
if you had to.

Dealing at the tables in Las Vegas,
the sixties, the lounge music so loud,
aspirin was called popcorn and the ears
haven't been right since. My kids hoot
at my miss-hears, all three ex wives
yelled at me to get a hearing aid,
which I won't because I've already got
enough old man shit going on.

I never understand the lyrics,
I can't hear the words. The voices
are just another instrument. That's why
now I love the opera, it's in Italian
or French, German, the 102-voice
chorus at the symphony, singing
in Latin, the Requiem, the music
loud enough to push through
the flattened cilia and the language
is just noise. The world
is a marvelous mush to me,
just sounds in the undifferentiated
space circling inside the bar,
street corner, espresso stand.

But the really important things
I can hear like, "Yes, I want
to go home with you", because
I can read her eyes and her hand's
gripping my thigh like a shark.

Double-wide

There is some God that hates the trailer parks, especially ones
with crummy names: the Rest-A-While, Lazy Palms, The Wagon Wheel,
especially on the edge of town, the county line, picks them first
before the rest. This God sets down twisters in their crowded midst,
rips them from their concrete pads, slings them around like kindling sticks,
sides split open like cans of corn, tattered, flapping insulation wrapped
around the upturned pickup trucks, the dinky pool filled with peoples' trash,
the laundry room hammered flat, the little rock lawns and concrete elves
and concrete crows buckshot up the spiral funnel cone. He fills them up
with drunken louts, chemistry labs, your only-on-Thanksgiving uncle and dogs
mean as Mondays. Why does He let the aliens abduct their owners,
Sissy and Jerell, Dustin and Krystal, beaming them to God knows where,
inserting robot body probes, sending them back to dither and swear the truth
on Channel Five: missing teeth, bushy brows. There is some God that hates
the trailer parks. God help me if they cut my retirement or raise my rent.
God help me if there's a double-wide in a crummy park on the road ahead.

The Older Guy Shops at Safeway

The self check out at the local food market
is a technology test in my neighborhood
which is a swarm of three-storey apartments
a free bus ride from the local university.
The market is in the middle, walkable
to the rentals, the line for beer sales
long at 10:30 Friday and Saturday nights.

These students are wired to their world,
phone to the ear, plastic food basket
in the other hand. They bang through
the robot cashier in a blur; scan
the bar code, price look-up,
no price code—find the product picture,
type in the frequent buyer club number,
swipe the debit card from their parents,
key in the pin number, pack it, bag it.
We all move like a Toyota assembly line.

Until

the geezer with the half glasses on a chain,
steps up, collared striped Polo shirt
tucked into his Bermuda shorts, black
knee high socks with dress shoes holding
a box of Dulcolax; there's grit in the gears.
The line is in trouble as he stares
at the display screen as though reading Greek.

I am embarrassed for my people. Those caught
with a typewriter in the study and a Princess phone
by the divan. Whoever told this guy dress shoes
went with shorts?

All the students in line turn and look at me
expecting more stripped gears. My God,
the pressure not to fuck up; a bottle of gin,
three limes, an avocado and a Mars bar;
I'm outta there in a minute thirty.
As I walk across the parking lot,
their cheers still ring in my ears.

Sometimes You Get What You Wish For

Nurse Mary burns the spot of pre cancerous cells
off my cheek for the second time, does the brown
spots on the back of my hand for free. I was about
to ask Nurse Mary to join me for a cappuccino
after work when she says, "My mother has the same
old age spots on her hands." I have clearly mistaken
her bedside manner for bedside manners. These
are the little messages God sends me. Like the agony
in the lower back and left shoulder mornings after
weight training. He hides my keys twice a week
so I won't forget Him. My last wife, amazingly
drenched with the spirit of Grace and Revelation
begged me to believe. "It's hard," I said, "When
He emails me, we'll see." That was a few years ago.
Nurse Mary reminds me that my full physical
is next month, throws over her shoulder as she leaves,
"Now I'll get to see ALL those tattoos of yours."
And I know He's fucking with me again.

John Cameron Swayze is Dead

The dog won't stop barking this morning
    as we wait at the rusty umbrella
        table for Ed, the recycle guy

who always has dog biscuits in his back pack.
    We're early. Twice a week
        we have coffee from the market,

talk about the stuff people throw away,
    poems I'm working on, family.
        I couldn't sleep. It's the beginning

of summer, my three part-time jobs
    have slowed down and I was worrying
        about all that free time

for the next three months. Free time
    as though other time has a price,
        like the cost of time thinking

about the new spot on your cheek,
    missing a birthday of one of your kids.
        Overslept my nap yesterday because

I messed up the alarm setting and missed
    happy hour, had to pay full price.
        When I graduated from high school,

fathers were still giving their children wrist watches
    for gifts. The symbol of serious intent, a hope
        the child would be that ordered person

who checks his wrist before leaving for class,
    lunch with the boss, getting to church.
        I broke mine in two weeks changing a tire

but still wore it so father would think
    I cared about time. At that time,
        time stretched as huge as a crop

of wheat. Maya Angelou died last Wednesday
    and poets everywhere are subtracting
        their age from her eighty-six to see

how much time there is left. For me, I have
    about fifteen. Some cultures consider time
        a banana; if you eat it, it's gone.

They have no word for yesterday or tomorrow.
    When you walk away, you're gone
        until you come back, unlike the dog

who knows Ed is late with the dog biscuit. A dog
    with a sense of time, a clock inside he picked
        up from me. Time doesn't have a cost,

it's a weight like a sack of rocks you have to carry,
    each year some punk puts another in the bag.
        If you swing the sack just right, the momentum

pulls you through another year. If not, it's curtains, rocks
    and rubble everywhere on the ground. You won't
        give a shit what time is or if Ed is late.

Gladstone's Eyes

The sky is the color of oxen, King Agamemnon says,
same as Ulysses' sea, described by Homer.

What ailed these people? No teal, aquamarine,
cerulean, tekelet, navy blue, for Christ's sake.

Why am I telling you this? Were the ancients
color blind? Color cones in the eyes Darwin's proof

of late stage evolution. Or, can something exist
if there are no words for it? Like tremendous

desire, or hopeless love poorly described in English
but beautiful in French, German. Does this mean

those people have lives so rich they invented words
to describe? The Arabs have one word for snow

and seventeen for the manner camels drink
from the water hole. Does this mean

when my first wife threw every dish on the floor
before leaving , she had no words to describe

absolute joy? And my father when he would slap me
up beside the head, it was because he was trying

to describe the magnitude of love?

JOSEPH AND THE MIRACLES

Adam

Adam is really tired, not just the job but all the questions: What was the garden like? How did the apple taste? Too bad about the son. Both he and Eve stay home, pull the curtains. It's easier to sit out on the back porch now that the hedge has grown so tall the neighbors can't see over. He can't believe he still has to go to work, but you know, there's the mortgage, car payments, helping the kids out; some are clever, some just don't get it, take Seth. Although God doesn't call, hasn't for decades, Adam recognizes His angels in unmarked cars that patrol his street. When he gets home from work there's usually one parked down the block, or walking a dog; really obvious. One even installed the cable. And the clothes, the business suit he has to wear, nothing like his old robe and sandals. On the weekend, he stands for a while in the grandkids' sandbox, wiggles his toes in the sand. It reminds him of the old days in the desert. Not like here in Seattle where he's been doing a kind of penance, all that mold and fog, it rained over two hundred eighty days last year. Forever just seems so far away.

Eve

Every week, Eve looks forward to getting her nails done, the Hmong women chirping to each other, call her "Missus." No one here seems to know who she is. No one blames her for everything. She leans back and lets the jabbering manicurist massage her hands. *If only Adam wasn't so old fashioned, I could get a job and have something to do,* Eve thinks. *Maybe work at Lillith's Busy Bee Bakery in the mornings; we've patched things up. Besides,* she thinks, *I'm really good at fruit.* She watches the guy with an umbrella and a shih tsu walk by the window for the third time. *A stupid angel,* she thinks. *They're always watching to make sure I don't fuck up again. So obvious, His angels, the pasty faces and bulky overcoats to cover their wings. It's so obvious.* Every now and then she lets them follow her into Pet Smart while she stares at the reptiles. *I shouldn't do this,* she thinks, *but it's so much fun.* The delicate young woman holding her hand leans close and whispers, "Okay, all done Missus Eve." Then winks. *I've got to get that bakery job,* Eve thinks, *I could do apple pies.*

Eve, again

I'm pissed, everyone is still blaming me for everything. Oh they've dressed it up in pious mythology but it's still blame. And Adam, he wanted that apple more than me, took it right out of my hand. He wanted to know what I looked like naked, liked the idea of looking under that leaf. And that snake, it was a man not a woman. A bit of a sleaze, thin moustache. But I knew what I was doing. I knew Adam was getting bored just wandering around in some new-age haze, not even paying much attention to the one job he had, naming things. Aardvark, for Christ's sake. Possum. Goldfish, now that's really inventive. And the jerk men have taken control of most everything since because HE said they could, even thank HIM every morning that HE didn't make them a woman. They wrap us up in yards of cloth because they can't trust their dicks; and blame us for that, blame ME for that. Or make us toddle around in ridiculous shoes, skirts up our butts, tits out to here carrying a purse big enough to hide a bushel of apples so we can't run away. Man up, suckers, admit it, ever since they invented seamed hose and thongs you've forgotten immortality, the pap of forever. Admit it, you'd have grabbed that apple out of my hand just to get a peek of pussy. And have been doing it ever since.

Noah

All day I watch for the anvil shaped clouds, the black roil, but there
is only the blue yarn of the sky, the sun dangling there, the neighbors
chippying around in the weeds. What do I do with this monster boat
if it's all bullshit? Maybe I just had too much mead and my wife and
kids were right, I'm crazy. Gopher wood HE said, only gopher wood.
That took forever. Half the world around here works for me, it's hard
and nasty work but they're mostly free to drink their wine at night;
all those animals in cages and pastures have to be fed, wagons of
fodder arrive every day and the manure, Oh Lord—excuse me—the
manure. The rhinoceroses are always watching the moon, skunks are
indifferent and bears are difficult to convince. If I don't keep everyone
apart, I have to find two more. There are no real instructions for what
HE wants. As long as that pile of thuya and gold keep appearing on
the table each morning, I can keep everything afloat, so to say. I don't
even have time to pray and HE's been on me about that too, *Noah,
don't forget the emus,* HE writes in the sky, *remember the weasels.
You haven't sacrificed anything to me in weeks.* If it doesn't rain
soon, I really will go crazy. And HE wants the bugs too, there's just
so many kinds. And only two flies, that's impossible. But I worry
about keeping the workers out of the boat after we load the animals.
I mean, a few of them don't seem a bad sort, but HE says no, they all
stay behind. *Bolt the doors, beat them off the sides with sticks, do
whatever.* I imagine the screams when the flood comes, the begging,
mothers holding up their little ones, take mine, take mine. How am
I going to live after that? Will it be enough that everything starts new
from here, from my three sons, from the two of everything? But how
will I live with the screams? When I ask HIM, there's no answer, just
writes on my forearm in black, *Get on with it.*

Joseph and the Miracles

Joseph eases the Studebaker around the close corners on the long dark road to Veazie, a sparse farm town on the Penobscot River, the plowed snow hunched like great dunes on each side of the road. Mary is wrapped in two shawls and wool socks because the heater is puny, she holds her hands around her great belly, humming to their soon, very soon, first child. He didn't want to drive all this way with her being so close, the threat of snow, the night so early, so cold but her parents called in the afternoon and asked them to come up for Christmas, the first time they reached out since they got married. A miracle, thinks Joseph, she picked me. I'm as old as her father. Been teaching wood shop at the high school for fifteen years. Only have an old clap board house I inherited from my uncle. Fresh out of Normal School to teach English, all the young guys bringing her coffee at the Monday morning teachers' meetings, and Mary picked me. She shifts in the seat, rubs her belly. It's hard to get comfortable when you're this big. That's the second miracle, Joseph thinks, the doctors told me I'd never have kids. The road weaves through scrub fields, the pine woods beyond their edges reach into the night, the frozen Penobscot a smooth desert on the right. Mary leans forward in the seat, grimaces. There hasn't been a place to turn around for miles and they're over half way there. Not many farms on this road and the few have all been dark, their driveways filled with drifts. The county plow goes by in the opposite direction. Ahead, set back off a long curved driveway, a two story house with its attached small barn is outlined with blue Christmas lights, a single tree, all blue, on the front lawn. A candle in each window and a bright white twinkling spotlight over the closed double doors to the barn. "Joe, honey. I think we better pull off here."

Three Men from Town

Three guys in a DeSoto fluid drive, the big pillow flakes turning to sleet, no traffic on the thin country road, no traffic but the county plow peeling the sleet into wet curls at the road edge. The coffee in the thermos ran out twenty miles south east. It's Christmas Eve, late. Their families, back in town, the trees decorated, fireplaces warming the living rooms, the wives are worried, a little angry. The guys couldn't tell them anything. They didn't know. Just called each other and agreed to meet at Gaspar's. Benny's wife wondered if there's someone else. They pull over to pee, leave the big DeSoto idling, stand around the tail lights and smoke a cigarette, overcoat collars turned up, fedoras catching the heavy sleet. It's Gaspar's car and his wife won't allow smoking inside. Gaspar, Mel and Benny; a doctor, owner of the town's hardware store and a fifth grade teacher, known each other since high school, football team, Gaspar on a battleship in the Pacific, Mel and Benny in Europe, two weeks after D-day. "Any idea where we're going, Gaspar?" Benny asks. Gaspar shrugs, "You know as much as I do." "I had this feeling," Mel says, "I should bring something." And pulls a small carved wooden sheep from his pocket. Gaspar shows them a small bottle of Balsam Oil, Benny has three candy canes tied with a ribbon. They all stare at the three gifts in the red glow of the tail lights, the sleet sticking to their shoulders. Gaspar flicks his cigarette in a sparkling comet over the snow drift at the edge of the road. "Let's keep going." The storm seems to be getting worse and Gaspar slows the DeSoto around the curves, its heater pushing the cold outside, the wipers barely keeping up. There are only a few farm houses alongside the road and they've all been dark, their driveways clogged with snow. Up ahead they see a blue glow on the deep snowy yard of a single house set back from the road. The house and attached barn are trimmed with only blue Christmas lights, a blue lit tree on the front lawn, a candle in each window. As they pull close the storm drops off and the moon burns the edges of a few white clouds in the dark sky. The moon is so bright they could drive without headlights. Over the barn door there is a bright twinkling spotlight, the only light not blue. The driveway is plowed clear. "I think this is it. I think we're here."

Emanuel

Manny was a handful for Joseph, asking questions he had never thought of, always saying things Joseph didn't understand. But Manny loved the woodshop, his dad's hands over his on the wood plane, the pine curls peeling in resin piles around their heads. And the auger, how to press your chest over the wood donut top, twirl the double U shaft and let the bit bite and chew its clean self through. School was a problem. Mary was called every month because Manny disrupted the class by asking the teacher why and not stopping if the teacher didn't know. On the way home from school, the loud, ecstatic frogs in spring were too much to ignore, the kids in his grade from North Orrington elementary would follow Manny to the over-swale of Sagadahok stream to watch him put his finger in the cold muck of a freshet, the nests of frog eggs, pills of tapioca balls each with a single eye dot. And the new frogs, fully grown, would rocket off in all directions. Do it again, they'd cheer. Until Zacchaeus, the farmer who owned the swale would run down in his frock coat and overalls, yelling to get to Hell off his land. The bigger boys at recess soon learned to leave Manny alone after he pointed at one kid's nose and it bled for a day, pointed at the worse one's leg after he pushed Manny off the swing. The school called Mary who hugged Manny close, whispered in his ear, kissed his tears and Zeno, the boy, could walk again. After four hours, Mary found his bike leaning against the side of the Grange Hall where the men were practicing for the installation of the new officers, all sitting in a circle around Manny as he asked them questions: How much is a soul worth? Where do sparrows go when they die if there are no sparrows in heaven? Why are some men's hearts good and others bad? Do you ever doubt? How are the Red Sox going to do next season? And that group of farmers, some in shitty boots and worn pants, leaning forward in their chairs, caps pushed back did their best to answer, did not lie. And Mary waited in the back, wept for her son. It wasn't easy, the raising, but they did it with help from the grandparents in Veazie, the annual summer month at the farm for Manny, slop the hogs, milk cows, tedding the hay, the chickens, mean geese, church every Sunday, the fourth of July softball game; Manny could catch but not hit. They loved this miracle grandson, the unexpected gift late in their lives. It was a long and difficult raising but Manny slowly increased in wisdom and stature and grace.

Luke 2:52

THE SHORT LIVES OF MEN

Memorial

For Anna DiMartino

I think of Grace, her ashes nibbled
by Garibaldi and sea bass after George
and his friends have sprinkled her
beyond the kelp beds. We're on the bluff
edge overlooking the soft rollers, behind us
windows in the big homes flash the late
afternoon sun. We are thinking of our souls
or at least how our ends will be, graceful
among family and friends or in the San Ysidro
Good Care Nursing Home, three to a room,
Lysol, bleach over urine and shit, the view
out the window a brick wall, parking lot
if you're lucky.

Grace's daughter, Anna, my friend, holds up.
She did her crying last night while George
held her. Under the warm breeze
on the bluff edge, she comforts the others,
has become the Great Mother as the bagpiper
in hot woolens, plays three tunes over and over
as George and his friends swim and paddle out
through the low surf to the kelp beds.

My friends love me but not like this family.
Sure, they'd meet at Pete's in La Mesa
for a pint of Fat Tire, a shot of so-so
bourbon and soon would start arguing
about the Republicans. But who
would swim out through the possible sharks?
They'd have to be rescued by lifeguards,
most would mix up the time or be late.

The best I can hope for is to check out quick,
arguing about Ireland with Cass, Scotland
with Steve, slobbering over the fifth beer
at the Sideways Bar, or gracefully stinking up
my one bedroom as the dog watches the door
and wonders about kibble. Better for everyone
if my ashes are pitched into the dumpster
behind 7-Eleven because I'll probably
be dropped by fumbling Doug on his way
to Grace's bluff, scuffed to the gutter,
the urn filled with dirt from a planter.

Promises

She's three
maybe four
corn silk hair
spraddle legged
between her dad's
on the skateboard
hands in his
clacking along
the sidewalk joints
on Adams Avenue
weaving between
the early bar crowd
serious
watching
where she's going
She'll always
remember these rides
when he gets home
early from work
the rift light
of October
Southern California
cool in the shadows
warm on the east side
of the street
She'll marry
a smart kid
with a blue parrot
tattooed on his chest
a ring in his nipple
Dad taught her
to do what
she likes
It's ok

The Short Lives of Men

At 3:15 Odin passed over, a red streak
above Napa Valley, Joel holding
his jowly head, now gray where the brick
red was. The mystical Odin who'd stare
at spirits in the wall for hours. And
I'm at my favorite dive, a thousand miles
south toasting the heavens with a shot
of rye, the other four guys and the barkeep,
Maddie, join in. Then one more for Bella,
the past Queen of Catahoula Hounds
in Eugene, ruler of the yard, escape artist,
benevolent disciplinarian of her brother
and all other dogs. It's been a tough year
for those hirsute saints who taught us
the fragile limits of being human, a primer
on pain, preparing us for the future
that streaks toward us, spitting, snarling
at our throats. I wear my dog sorrow
poorly, a ratty coat in winter. There is
a constant replenishing of the empty
dog-soul gaps with other pups
who struggle up the scree to our hearts,
but there's always a nail hole in the soul
that refuses the caulk. I will not be consoled.
I want the warm West Coast of before,
the red dog red, Bella in charge and me miles
from the end these beauties remind me is coming.

A Taste of Time

The three come into the Aero Club
blinking like owls, the light to dark
is tough on old eyes. Squinting
at the barkeep, the guy bald
as a rock says, "Three tequila
shots, please." The woman,
sparrow after a thin winter,
sits between them, they lean
into her and stare like when
she was twenty. "Lime, Please."
And she is twenty again, and so
are they. She coughs into her hand
and the guys look at each other
over her dipped head. "Cheers."
Up go the elbows and down slips
the memory; bite the lime.
She smiles at each guy, kisses
the one on the left, then
the right. They help her off
the stool and hold the door open.
A float of the perfume Opium
from her red scarf drifts down
the bar from the closing door.

Patience

If I had written this poem when I was younger,
about a guy alone in the Aero Club, probably retired
or at least out of work, two-thirty in the afternoon,
the pint of craft beer, the caramel colored bourbon
blinking in the sliced light from the overhead fan,
I'd have got it all wrong.

I would have imagined he had just a couple of bucks
in his pocket. No one at home except the cat and cat box.
The rooms small. But I have waited to write this,
because the Aero Club just opened for the day.
No one's here yet. Barbara pulls down her shorts
to show me her new tattoo. Something she'd never
have done if I was twenty-one, no job, at two-thirty
with a beer and a shot.

Last Seen 18 June

Mac is missing. Someone left the slider open. Too much
for a cat to resist even if Mac has never been much outside.

And past the agapanthus, has no idea where he is. *Domestic*
shorthair, age 10. Reward, call Kathy. Friendly toward humans

and dogs but don't try to pick him up. Mac is black with large
green eyes. Please call ASAP. It's been three weeks, the flyers

are ripped and faded on the lamp poles. We are changed forever
when the cat leaves. Not in extravagance but in some small dark pit.

Not like seeing the polar cap of Mars through the big telescope
in Berkeley, the room of Van Goghs in the Jeu de Paume, Jeannie

Balabus after the junior prom, not like that but moth like, a prickle
of arm hair. Leaving Maine in the fifties was a lot like Mac

and the open slider, no idea where I was going, roaming strange nights
for years, no one to hang a flyer for me. One day management

will clean out my place, replace the carpet, clean behind the stove
and someone somewhere will be changed a bit. In that small dark pit,

Mac and I will eye each other, being sure not to pick him up.

Whoa

I saw my father last week. He looked younger
    than when he died. It was at my favorite bar,

the one with twenty-two craft beers on tap
    which was a worry because he never drank.

How's mom, I asked. "Super. She's at
    her Zumba class." He holds his glass up

to the light, the deep honey hue sparkles.
    "You know, I'd of had a drink if they'd had

this good stuff back then. We eat sushi now,
    every Wednesday. Imagine that. Us two

old shits from Maine." Shakes a Chesterfield
    from the pack in his pocket. "You can smoke there."

He winks at me. "It doesn't make any difference. I hear
    you're gonna visit us soon. Come by on Wednesdays."

Who gets the books and CDs

I live alone with the dog who's eight
has seven or so years left

which means
I'll be alone when losing the keys

means much more than now

who will notice the brain turning butter
not me

I'll be too close to the whole thing

maybe some neighbor will call the cops
my CD of Purcell's Dido and Aeneas

on repeat for three days
volume too high

outside
in my boxers feeling the eucalyptus bark

except for the occasional flicker
a Perseid streak in November

I won't care
won't even know it's me

The National League Playoffs
are a Form of Self Pity

Every now and then, usually in the low light
of summer nights, perhaps the breeze
whiffing jasmine through the window,
and on the radio, the Giants play the Dodgers,
the low voices a narcotic murmur, the family
in the living room watching TV, I think about,
or, like tonight, read about, my other life,
the one left somewhat behind but maybe
not really that far behind because it hurts
so much to think of it, or read about.
An ex-wife prints an interview
of another poet who read with her
at the 42nd Street "Y" in Manhattan,
a poetry Mecca of sorts, introduced
by Jack Gilbert, a Pharaoh, a poet
Essene who used to be someone
I drank tea with, strolled in Golden
Gate Park and discussed why we did this,
this poetry. But not anymore. Divorce
divides, not just the children, the books
and pets, but the Gurus, the future.
We make our choices and I can't fault mine.
I sit at the dinner table most nights,
her children, sticky faced and laughing
at the other end and talk of sixth grade
and kindergarten. We talk about the weekend
when the ex gets the kids and we have the house
to ourselves, don't lock the bedroom door.
We talk about all there is to a life
that plots a safe green field for three
kids and two adults to grow in.

The Giants gamble with the hit and run,
Pablo Sandoval gets tagged at third,
and I flinch—like at the end of a great poem,
like the end of an evening at the Mondavi
Winery long ago when Jack, a dim light
haloing his head, read and read in the
slippery hot night and we wouldn't let
him stop.

Double Play

She's five seats over, alone
with a glove and score card.
The stands are empty,
the team's in the cellar,
season almost over,
the players trying hard
to appear interested,
worth their pay.
We're all waiting
for next season.

When the foul ball arcs
toward her, she stretches
with her glove, score card,
water bottle, seat pad,
peanuts, ball cap flying.
She's not the youngster
we first thought,
got many seasons behind her,
but still on the team.

My friend leaps to help,
hitches up his jeans,
gold chain nestled in the gray
barbed wire exposed chest,
smooths his team shirt
with "Gonzales" on the back
over his rubber waist,
looks back at me,
"Can o'corn," he says.

Requiem

Fern and Claire settle in,
seats at the third balcony edge,
just third base side of home plate
so lefty fouls come their way.
Each have their husband's old glove,
soft with neatsfoot oil, although Claire
has been known to use mayonnaise.
Sun visors, blockout, water bottles,
program, cheese sandwiches
and apple wedges. A sweater
in case the fog rolls in. These are
day games now, it's just too tough
to get to the park at night.

Fern fills out the score card
but needs Claire whose eyes are better,
two shelves at home filled with cards
going back to when the boys were alive.
It used to be season tickets but after
the new stadium and price hikes,
it was only the day games. Then when
the free agent pitcher blew out
his arm and that big stick gamble
at first ripped his Achilles, the prices
went up again and now it's only
a couple of twelve pack deals twice
a season. They get together and listen
to the missed games on the radio,
Ted Lightner cracking jokes; it's harder
for Fern to keep score. But nothing
changes, the Padres live in the cellar,
trade the guy a year before his break-out,

sell the only bat over three hundred
before free agency. Second lowest
salary in the majors and Fern and Claire
still bleed Padre Blue.

When the boys were alive
it was a week in Phoenix each year
—spring training—The Pony Bar
in Scottsdale after the games,
meeting the rookies, a few old pros.

Now it's only Fern and Claire and
the Padres losing year after year:
new owners and it's still the cellar.

When the latest savior wiffs
on three pitches, Claire levers
herself up with the balcony rail,
her voice clear to center field,
"Hurry up, you sons-a-bitches,
we haven't got that much time left."

Passover at the Ballpark

Sundown on Friday,
a confluence of issues
and I'm torn between
opening day and the Seder,
the bread prayers, salt,
horseradish, the stories
by the youngest at the table.
But, it's opening night, we've got
a new pitcher, a new stick
in left field, maybe
this is our year. Sandy Koufax
would understand, so would
Hank Greenberg, but
my long dead grandmother
is another story. I feel
her sitting in the seat
just behind me, imagining
the kippah beneath
my ball cap, babushka
knotted tight under her chin,
hissing between her teeth
as I elbow the guy beside me
and leap with my glove
for the foul ball.